Faithbuilders Bible Studies

The Prophecy of Amos

A Warning for Today

by Mathew Bartlett

The Prophecy of Amos: A Warning for Today by Mathew Bartlett

First Published in Great Britain in 2015

FAITHBUILDERS PUBLISHING www.biblestudiesonline.org.uk

An Imprint of Apostolos Publishing Ltd,
3rd Floor, 207 Regent Street,
London W1B 3HH
www.apostolos-publishing.com

Copyright © 2015 Mathew Bartlett & Derek Williams.

All rights reserved. No part of this book may be reproduced or transmitted in any form or by any means, electronic or mechanical, including photocopying, recording, or by any information storage and retrieval system, without permission in writing from the publisher.

Unless otherwise indicated, the Scripture quotations contained herein are from the New Revised Standard Version Bible, copyright © 1989, by the Division of Christian Education of the National Council of the Churches of Christ in the U.S.A., and are used by permission. All rights reserved.

Scripture quotations marked "NKJV™" are taken from the New King James Version®. Copyright © 1982 by Thomas Nelson, Inc. Used by permission. All rights reserved.

British Library Cataloguing-in-Publication Data

A catalogue record for this book is available from the British Library

ISBN: 978-1-910942-19-2

Cover Design by Blitz Media, Pontypool, Torfaen

Cover Image © Designpicssub | Dreamstime Stock Photos

Printed and bound in Great Britain by Marston Book Services Limited, Oxfordshire.

Dedicated to all those who are hungry for God's Word.

More from Faithbuilders Bible Studies

Faithbuilders Bible studies: Matthew

Faithbuilders Bible studies: Mark

Esther – Queen of Persia

Zechariah – Prophet of Messiah

Contents

Amos 1:1–2:3 Judgment on the Nations 7

    Introduction 7

    God's Judgment Imminent 8

    Judgments Against: Syria 9

    Philistia 11

    Tyre 11

    Edom 12

    Ammon 13

    Moab 14

Amos 2:4–16 Judgment on Judah and Israel 16

    Judgment Against Judah 16

    Judgment Against Israel 17

        Heartless Oppression of the Poor 17

        Perverted Justice 18

        Sexual Immorality and Idolatry 19

        God Rejected 20

        Judgment Unavoidable 22

Amos 3:1–15. The Broken Covenant 25

    A Broken Covenant 25

    The Prophet Defends His Office 26

    A Remnant Will be Saved 29

Amos 4:1–13. Hypocritical Religion 33

Punishment for "Fat Cows" 33

Religious Pride and Hypocrisy 34

God's Dealings to Israel to Repentance 35

Final Judgment is Inevitable 37

Amos 5:1–27. A Lament for the Nation 39

A Lament for the Nation 39

Seek God in Truth 41

A Promise for the Repentant 45

The Day of the Lord 45

Sincerity in Worship 47

Amos 6:1–14. Warning to the Unconcerned 51

A Warning to the Unconcerned 51

Pride and Selfish Indulgence 52

The Severity of the Coming Judgment 55

Amos 7:1–17. Intercession and Opposition 57

Intercession for Israel 57

The Vision of Locusts 57

The Vision of a Destroying Fire 57

The Vision of the Plumb Line 58

Opposition to the Word of God 59

Amos Threatened 60

Amos Defends His Ministry 60

Amos Stands for the Truth 62

    Amaziah's Punishment.. 62

Amos 8:1–14. The Basket of Ripe Summer Fruit................................ 63

    A Basket of Ripe Summer Fruit 63

    A Warning of Judgment 64

Amos 9:1–15. No Escape—But a Saviour Promised 71

    The Temple at Bethel Destroyed 71

    No Escape From God's Judgment 72

    Misplaced Trust 74

    Scattering and Sifting 75

    The Restoration of the Davidic Kingship 76

Amos 1:1–2:3 Judgment on the Nations

Introduction

1:1 The words of Amos, who was among the shepherds of Tekoa, which he saw concerning Israel in the days of King Uzziah of Judah and in the days of King Jeroboam son of Joash of Israel, two years before the earthquake.

Very little is known about the prophet Amos other than what is written here; that he worked "among the shepherds" in the area of Tekoa. The word translated "shepherds" can refer to various kinds of livestock and it is by no means clear whether Amos was the owner of the livestock or just a hired hand. Not much is known of Tekoa, either, except that is was a town in Southern Judah, near Bethlehem. It was fortified by Rehoboam *(2 Chron. 11:6)* and surrounded by rocky desert *(2 Chron. 20:20).*

God's choice of Amos shows how God calls the weak and ordinary instead of the wise and strong *(1 Cor. 1:26–27).* Amos was a nobody, but God revealed Himself to Amos through His word, just as today He reveals Himself to all who put their faith in His Son, the Lord Jesus Christ.

The vision Amos received warned of God's judgment on many nations, but especially Israel, which by the time of Amos' ministry had already been split into two kingdoms - Israel and Judah. This happened when ten tribes of Israel rebelled against Solomon's son Rehoboam and made Jeroboam king over them, taking for themselves the name Israel. Only Judah and Benjamin remained faithful to Rehoboam, David's grandson, and his realm then adopted the name Judah. That is why the two kingdoms are referred to separately throughout the book of Amos, who prophesied during the reigns of Uzziah king of Judah and Jeroboam II king of Israel (who, according to Thiele, reigned between 782 and 753 BCE). This made him a contemporary of Isaiah and Hosea. The exact time when his message was given is said to be "two years before the earthquake". This must have been an event of some significance to be used as a date marker by the compiler of Amos' prophecies. Unfortunately, today we cannot be certain as to its exact date.

God's Judgment Imminent

> *1:2 And he said: The LORD roars from Zion, and utters his voice from Jerusalem; the pastures of the shepherds wither, and the top of Carmel dries up.*

Amos warns his hearers of impending judgment. A lion does not roar unless it has a prey. Israel is the prey that God is about to take in judgment. The picture of God making his voice heard from Jerusalem, the place which He had appointed for worship, is significant, since under the leadership of Jeroboam I, Israel had forsaken this place of worship and instead worshipped the golden calves at Bethel and Dan. Jeroboam had even appointed his own priests, contrary to God's command. This entire system of idolatry was designed by Jeroboam to prevent his subjects being reunited with Judah. He reasoned, quite shrewdly, that if the people had the same religion and worshipped in the same place, then a national reunion, based on repentance toward God, would be more likely to occur *(1 Kings 12:26–33).* Although God had given ten tribes to Jeroboam as a punishment on David's family because of their idolatry in the days of Solomon, He was further angered when Jeroboam began to follow the same ways as the King who was ousted before him. God's judgment on the idolatrous nation was sure to come, and would initially take the form of a drought, which would result in a lack of pasture for sheep. Israel was known as a nation of shepherds, but as a consequence of the drought, even the lush pasture of Carmel would wither, for God had warned Israel that if they were unfaithful to Him then: *The LORD will change the rain of your land into powder, and only dust shall come down upon you from the sky until you are destroyed (Deut. 28:24).*

Judgments Against: Syria

1:3 Thus says the LORD: For three transgressions of Damascus, and for four, I will not revoke the punishment; because they have threshed Gilead with threshing sledges of iron.

Amos now begins to pronounce judgment on the five nations surrounding Israel. The formula "for three... for four" shows how these nations continued obstinately in their evil ways, for if a nation had seen it's error, they may have repented and God would not need to speak of judgment. But the verses reveal an absence of repentance. As a result of the nations' persistent sin, God says to each one, "I will not turn away" - judgment could no longer be withheld.

First to be dealt with is Syria. Damascus, the capital of Syria, represents the rule of the nation and therefore denotes the nation as a whole. Gilead was near Syria and seems to have been a regular target for Syrian troops *(see 2 Kings 10:32–33)*. Although it is true that God had used Syria to chastise unfaithful Israel, they would not be excused for their inhumanity. The Israelites which the Syrians captured in battle were literally threshed to death with farming implements of sharpened metal ("threshing sledges of iron"). For this war crime God would judge the whole Syrian nation.

1:4 So I will send a fire on the house of Hazael, and it shall devour the strongholds of Ben-hadad.

Hazael and Ben-Hadad had both been kings of Syria and so represent the rulers of that nation. As Tatford points out, the name "Ben-Hadad" was adopted by many Syrian kings in honour of their god "Hadad", the god of storms ("Ben-Hadad" means "son of Hadad"). The fire, symbolic of God's judgment, would come to destroy their rule and ruin their nation. Throughout Amos' prophecy, it is the fire of war. Many towns and cities were literally burned to the ground by invading armies.

> 1:5 I will break the gate bars of Damascus, and cut off the inhabitants from the Valley of Aven, and the one who holds the scepter from Beth-eden; and the people of Aram shall go into exile to Kir, says the LORD.

The capital, Damascus, would be besieged before eventually being captured (this is symbolised by the broken gate bar) and there would be no one left in the whole country of Syria, from "the Valley of Aven to Beth Eden" indicates that the conquest would be all inclusive. In Britain we might use the phrase "from Lands' End to John O'Groats", meaning the whole nation.

In days when Assyria was not considered big enough to pose a threat to the surrounding countries, Amos accurately predicted the Assyrian invasion of Syria. The victorious invaders literally deported the whole Syrian nation, rulers and subjects (that is, "the inhabitants" and "he that holds the scepter"), and resettled them elsewhere, as was their usual policy with prisoners of war. The place of their resettlement is named as Kir. There is considerable debate among scholars as to which city is meant, for the word "Kir" simply means "a walled enclosure" and more than one city of that time was named "Kir".

However, what is clear is that only thirty years after Amos uttered his prophecy, it was fulfilled *(2 Kings 16:9)*.

Philistia

> *1:6–8 Thus says the LORD: For three transgressions of Gaza, and for four, I will not revoke the punishment; because they carried into exile entire communities, to hand them over to Edom. So I will send a fire on the wall of Gaza, fire that shall devour its strongholds. I will cut off the inhabitants from Ashdod, and the one who holds the scepter from Ashkelon; I will turn my hand against Ekron, and the remnant of the Philistines shall perish, says the Lord GOD.*

Philistia is next to come under Divine sentence and is symbolised by its chief city of Gaza. The Philistines were to be judged for their part in the deporting of an entire population, possibly from a region of Israel. Those they took as captives were, says Tatford, presumably sold as slaves to the Edomites. (Edom was a nation which traded in slaves; *see 2 Chronicles 28:17*). The judgment of God coming upon the wall indicates that there would be no protection for the city from its high towers and fortifications, which would be destroyed.

Philistia was not in fact a nation but a federation of city kingdoms, each with its own king. All but one of these cities (Ashdod, Ashkelon, Ekron and Gaza) are named here, each city and king receiving their share of the judgment. Only Gath is not mentioned, though it is not excluded, since God makes clear that the whole population (remnant - whoever is left) of the Philistines would perish.

Tyre

> *1:9–10 Thus says the LORD: For three transgressions of Tyre, and for four, I will not revoke the punishment; because they*

> *delivered entire communities over to Edom, and did not remember the covenant of kinship. So I will send a fire on the wall of Tyre, fire that shall devour its strongholds.*

Tyre was a shipping port in Phoenicia. It is unlikely that they captured men as slaves, but rather that they traded in the Jewish slaves which were captured by the Philistines. They were middlemen, selling the slaves on to Edom. God's case against them is that they should not have shut their eyes to the suffering of these Jews, but they should have remembered the peace treaty which their nation, under king Hiram, had made with Israel at the time of King Solomon *(1 Kings 5:12)*. As was the case with Gaza, walls and fortifications could provide no protection from the judgment of God. This is why the Psalmist sang, *"Unless the Lord guards the city, the guard keeps watch in vain." (Psalm 127:1).* Today in Western Countries we pride ourselves in our ability to wage high tech warfare and for security we trust our "nuclear deterrent". The message of Amos abides that men ought not to trust in defences, but in God, who is able to make any defence as naught before His judgment.

Edom

> *1:11–12 Thus says the LORD: For three transgressions of Edom, and for four, I will not revoke the punishment; because he pursued his brother with the sword and cast off all pity; he maintained his anger perpetually, and kept his wrath forever. So I will send a fire on Teman, and it shall devour the strongholds of Bozrah.*

Next comes judgment on Edom. The Edomites were descendants of Esau, Jacob's older brother, and should have shown some affection for their relatives the Jews. The opposite was true. They manifested continual hostility to Israel, an unreasonable hatred which allowed no mercy or pity, a cruel anger which was never satisfied by any amount of vengeance. Like the men Paul describes, they were *"without natural affection." (2 Tim. 3:3).*

Since no further elaboration is made about Edom's judgment, the "fire in Teman" that would "devour Bozrah" must refer to events similar to those depicted in the previous prophecies - that is, Assyrian and later Babylonian invasions decimating the entire nation.

Ammon

> *1:13 Thus says the LORD: For three transgressions of the Ammonites, and for four, I will not revoke the punishment; because they have ripped open pregnant women in Gilead in order to enlarge their territory.*

The Ammonites were a very cruel people. Their soldiers deliberately targeted pregnant woman and cut them open in order to kill mother and child. They had no mercy in their lust to gain more land. Gilead, an extensive and mountainous region of Israel, which was close to the Ammonite border, was seized by them in this way.

> *1:14–15 So I will kindle a fire against the wall of Rabbah, fire that shall devour its strongholds, with shouting on the day of battle, with a storm on the day of the whirlwind; then their king shall go into exile, he and his officials together, says the LORD.*

The same fate of defeat in battle and subsequent captivity awaited Ammon and its rulers as did Syria and its rulers, coming suddenly and irresistibly like a whirlwind. Ray Beeley says, *"According to Poole, (this) judgment was eventually completed by the Babylonians."* (cf. Ezekiel 25:1–4).

Moab

> *2:1 Thus says the LORD: For three transgressions of Moab, and for four, I will not revoke the punishment; because he burned to lime the bones of the king of Edom.*

Such was the violent nature of the Moabites that they were not content merely to kill the King of Edom; they dissolved his bones in lime. No respect was shown for man, who is created in the image of God, not even for the human body after death. This crime may have had special significance if, as Tatford suggests, it was done as an offering to one of their gods.

> *2:2–3 So I will send a fire on Moab, and it shall devour the strongholds of Kerioth, and Moab shall die amid uproar, amid shouting and the sound of the trumpet; I will cut off the ruler from its midst, and will kill all its officials with him, says the LORD.*

Kerioth was the capital city of Moab. War and violent destruction would overtake the land (advancing armies are indicated by the sound of the trumpet) and all the leaders, whether judges or princes, would be killed.

So ends Amos' pronunciation of judgment on the heathen nations surrounding Israel. These were people who neither knew God nor worshipped Him. God nevertheless held them accountable for their actions. The apostle Paul in his letter to the Romans points out that such people will be judged according to the light which they have received, in particular that revelation of God's eternal power and Godhead which is self-evident in creation. This is so sufficient and compelling evidence as to leave even those who do not have the scriptures without any excuse for their rejection of God.

> *For what can be known about God is plain to them, because God has shown it to them. Ever since the creation of the world his eternal power and Divine nature, invisible though they are, have been understood and seen through the things He has made. So they are without excuse (Rom. 1:19–20)*

The God who was at work in Amos' day to bring judgment on the heathen is still in charge of world affairs today, governing the nations. All nations would do well to realise that it is not through strength of arms, nor use of force, but in dependence on God that true national security lies.

God is not only the God of nations, but of every individual. The day is coming when God shall judge every person for their own sins *(Acts 17:31)*. The verdict of this future and final judgment will depend on whether or not a person has received the Lord Jesus Christ as their Saviour. Only those who do so will escape the wrath of God *(John 3:36; 1 Thessalonians 1:10)* and eternal punishment *(Hebrews 6:2)*.

If those who did not know God and did not have His word were judged just as Amos foretold, what would happen to those who knew God's word and yet rejected it? Amos next turns his attention to those who were privileged to possess God's word yet were failing to obey it - Israel and Judah.

Amos 2:4–16 Judgment on Judah and Israel

Having pronounced judgment on the surrounding nations, Amos turns his attention to God's own people: Judah (vv. 4–5) and Israel (vv. 6–16).

Judgment Against Judah

> 2:4 Thus says the LORD: For three transgressions of Judah, and for four, I will not revoke the punishment; because they have rejected the law of the LORD, and have not kept his statutes, but they have been led astray by the same lies after which their ancestors walked.

The people of Judah were privileged to have the Scriptures in their possession. Not only had God given them His word but throughout their history He had provided them with priests, prophets and teachers to interpret His word and instruct them in it, so that they were without excuse. Greater privileges bring greater responsibilities *(Romans 2:11–12)*. Although Judah had the law, they had broken it and rejected the truth they had received. Rather than treat God's word with respect by careful study and obedience, they made light of it, as if it were an irrelevance.

Judah decided to go their own way and listen to their own hearts, exchanging the worship of the true God for that of idols, "their lies" *(see Romans 1:23)*. This is exactly what their forefathers had done when they rejected God and chose to worship a calf of gold they had made for themselves. Even as Christians, we may at times insist on our own will rather than obey God. This is the very basis of idolatry *(1 Samuel 15:23)*. We may not have idols of gold or silver, but following our own hearts is allowing ourselves to be deceived. The end of that way is death *(Proverbs 14:12)*.

> 2:5 So I will send a fire on Judah, and it shall devour the strongholds of Jerusalem.

God's threatened judgment was a long time in coming, for He was very patient and gave opportunity for the people to repent. Yet reforms during the days of Hezekiah and Josiah were not sufficient to avert the judgment. Less than 200 years after Amos had prophesied, the Babylonians came and literally burned Jerusalem with fire *(Nehemiah 1:3; 2 Chronicles 36:14–21).*

Amos now moves on to the major theme of his message, the judgment of the northern kingdom of Israel.

Judgment Against Israel

God's judgment against Israel was imminent for the following reasons:

Heartless Oppression of the Poor

> 2:6 Thus says the LORD: For three transgressions of Israel, and for four, I will not revoke the punishment; because they sell the righteous for silver, and the needy for a pair of sandals--

Israel's wealthy rulers had ordered the poor to be sold as slaves in order to pay their debts, contrary to Divine law. As Frederick Taford says, "*The law allowed a poor Hebrew to sell himself into slavery for six years (Deuteronomy 15:12) ... but it gave no power to enable creditors to sell an insolvent debtor."* The poor were not at fault - the word "righteous" as used here means they were not guilty of wrongdoing. They had been forced to borrow money in order to survive. The small size of the debts illustrates the implacability of the leaders - they had no mercy on their brothers. Silver was not as valuable as gold, and the poor were reduced to slavery for the repayment of a debt worth a pair of sandals. Such practices remained common in New Testament times

(James 5:1 - 6). It is in this context that our Lord warned that no mercy will be shown to the merciless *(James 2:13)*.

> *2:7 They pant after the dust of the earth which is on the head of the poor... (NJKV™).*

So that they might get rich quick and keep themselves in ever increasing luxury the rich "trampled on the heads of the poor". It could be said today that directors and shareholders of companies who get rich on the backs of ill-paid workers living in countries where there is little or no social or health care provision fall under the same condemnation. The law of God places a clear responsibility on employers to pay a fair wage for the work that is done for them. James declares: *"The wages of the labourers who mowed your fields, which you kept back by fraud, cry out, and the cries of the harvesters have reached the ears of the Lord of hosts." (James 5:4)*

For the "fat cats" to get fatter whilst the poor are reduced to slavery is a violation not merely of human rights, but of Divine law.

Perverted Justice

> *7. ...and pervert the way of the humble. (NKJV™).*

Amos's words imply that judges were accepting bribes to give favourable judgments to the rich against the poor so that they might make further financial gains.

Humility is a characteristic which is despised by every proud heart. The humble were not accepted as part of the "in crowd" and were denied basic rights and justice. Today, as in Amos' time, the proud are exalted among men, or as Malachi put it "we call the proud blessed." *(Malachi 3:15)*.

Sexual Immorality and Idolatry

> 7. *A man and his father go in to the same girl, To defile My holy name. (NKJV™).*

Next on Amos' list of indictments is sexual immorality, which became rife in Israel largely due to its link with their pagan system of worship (idolatry). As part of their "worship" to the pagan gods of fertility, the men of Israel paid for sexual intercourse with prostitutes in the idols' temples. By doing so they hoped to evoke the favour of that particular god and perhaps ensure a good harvest. God's law made clear that a man should not have a sexual relationship with the same woman as his father *(Deuteronomy 22:30)*. Yet this was happening, probably in the idol temples. The same thing happened in the Corinthian church, which failed to discipline the person involved, forcing the apostle Paul to intervene *(1 Corinthians 5:1)*. Paul taught that rather than defile God's name by using our bodies (which are the temples of the Holy Spirit) for sexual sin, we should use them to glorify God *(1 Corinthians 6:18–20)*.

If our view of the relationship between man and woman is lowered from God's standard, then our concept of the Creator also becomes lowered. Ray Beeley says, *"A low view of womanhood is related to a low view of God. It is only when men and women are reconciled to God that they truly appreciate the sanctity of sex. The relationship between man and wife described in Ephesians 5:22–35 is based on the Christian experience of reconciliation."*

> *2:8 they lay themselves down beside every altar on garments taken in pledge; and in the house of their God they drink wine bought with fines they imposed.*

In the law, Moses permitted an outer garment to be taken as a deposit against a loan made to someone. However, since the borrower would be poor, the cloak was to be returned by nightfall, as it was the only covering they had to keep them warm at night. *(Exodus 22:26).* This law was to be followed whether the loan had been repaid or not. Not only were these garments being kept by money lenders but they were laid down beside the altars of Israel's pagan shrines that on them they might indulge in sexual relations with the temple prostitutes.

Wine was accepted as payment of fines in the law courts and was to have been the property of the Levites. Israel, however, had appointed their own priests and as part of their idolatrous worship they drank this wine to their gods in the shrines they had built. The New Testament warns against drink *(Ephesians 5:18);* idolatry *(1 Corinthians 10:14–21);* and sexual immorality *(1 Corinthians 6:18).*

God Rejected

> *2:9 Yet I destroyed the Amorite before them, whose height was like the height of cedars, and who was as strong as oaks; I destroyed his fruit above, and his roots beneath.*

The people of Israel should have been thankful to God. He had given them the land in which they lived by destroying a much stronger nation before them—the Amorites—totally wiping them out, root and fruit.

> *2:10 Also I brought you up out of the land of Egypt, and led you forty years in the wilderness, to possess the land of the Amorite.*

God Himself had brought Israel out of slavery in Egypt and had remained faithful to them during their years of disobedience in the desert. He fed and provided for them in order to keep His promise to give them the land. The reference to the Exodus and subsequent settlement of the promised land of Canaan was a reminder to the nation that God had acted in history to bring them into a relationship with Himself. He had not done this because they merited His notice, but by His own choice, by grace. The charge against them is that by their deliberate rejection of God they were repudiating what He had done for them. This is significant, since as they had rejected Him who gave them the land, so when His judgment fell their land would be forfeited.

> *2:11 And I raised up some of your children to be prophets and some of your youths to be nazirites. Is it not indeed so, O people of Israel? says the LORD.*

God had chosen men from among His people to be priests, prophets and holy men (Nazirites) so that Israel might learn to obey His word. Even when backslidden, Israel was not able to deny this. They were not backslidden due to a lack of patient instruction, but in spite of it.

> *2:12 But you made the nazirites drink wine, and commanded the prophets, saying, "You shall not prophesy."*

In spite of all He had done for them, the people of Israel did not honour God, instead they turned their backs on Him and disregarded His commands. They showed contempt for holy things and for the vow of separation by forcing those who had made vows to break them (a Nazarite vowed not to drink wine) and by forbidding the prophets to speak in God's name. They simply could not bear to hear godly teaching nor to see godly example. They wanted to remove all traces of God from their lives. They preferred sin to repentance and so rejected God's gift of life, as many people still do today *(John 3:19)*. To such people God is merely a burden they wish to be rid of, His law a chain upon their conscience from which they wish to break free.

The prominence given today to those who deny the existence of God through the theory of evolution is an indication, not so much of advancement in science and education, but of the same sinful desire to be free from all moral obligations to the Creator.

Judgment Unavoidable

> 2:13 Behold, I am weighed down by you, As a cart full of sheaves is weighed down. (NKJV™).

If God is a burden to the people, they are a burden to Him. He is weary of putting up with them. For although God is patient, He is also holy, and will not endure man's sin forever. God compares Himself to a cart, groaning and creaking because it is overloaded with corn. Since He is overloaded with the sin of the people, God will not restrain His wrath any longer. Judgment is inevitable.

> :14 Flight shall perish from the swift, and the strong shall not retain their strength, nor shall the mighty save their lives;

The judgment about to fall will be unavoidable. There will be no escape for the swift. Both speed and strength shall be useless. Even the strongest men will not be able to survive the force of the coming onslaught.

> 2:15 those who handle the bow shall not stand, and those who are swift of foot shall not save themselves, nor shall those who ride horses save their lives;

The armed will not be able to defend themselves against the coming judgment. The fastest runners and those on horseback shall not be able to escape it. Since this judgment has been ordained by God, no mere man shall be able, by any means whatever, to elude His purpose.

> *2:16 The most courageous men of might Shall flee naked in that day, Says the Lord. (NKJV™).*

The judgment will be so severe that the bravest fighting men will run away in sheer terror, leaving even their clothes behind them. This could possibly indicate a surprise attack, where Israel's men were awakened from sleep and forced to flee without having time to dress.

In our day, too, God is patient. Since He is not willing for any to perish, He is holding back the judgment we deserve in order to give opportunity for all men to believe the gospel and be saved. But this day of opportunity will end. God's judgment will be poured out on the earth, and the unrepentant shall suffer dreadful and inescapable punishment in the lake of fire *(Revelation 20:15)*.

No one can escape this, even by dying, for *"it is appointed for men to die once, but after this the judgment" (Hebrews 9:27)*. When John the Baptist warned men to *"flee from the wrath to come"* he told them of One who is the God given means of escape, the Lord Jesus Christ who *"saves us from the wrath to come" (1 Thessalonians 1:10)*.

God's judgment of the nations of today will come as surely as that which was predicted by Amos. Pusey (cited by Tatford, 1974) shows how Amos prophecy was fulfilled over a period of time by the invasions of Assyrian emperors Tilgath-Pilesar (c. 745–727 BCE) and Sargon II (c. 722–705 BCE); the Babylonian emperor Nebuchadnezzar (c. 634–562 BCE) and much later by Alexander the Great (c. 356–323 BCE).

"There followed, under Tilgath-Pilesar, the fulfilment of the prophecy as to Damascus and Gilead. Under Sargon was fulfilled the prophecy on the ten tribes. That on Judah yet waited 133 years and was then fulfilled by Nebuchadnezzar. A few years later, and he executed God's judgments foretold by Amos on their enemies Moab, Ammon, Edom, Tyre. Kings of Egypt, Assyria and the Macedonian Alexander fulfilled in succession the prophecy as to Philistia."

God's actions in history should serve as a warning for today since neither He nor His standards ever change.

Amos 3:1–15. The Broken Covenant

A Broken Covenant

> 3:1 Hear this word that the LORD has spoken against you, O people of Israel, against the whole family that I brought up out of the land of Egypt:

Whilst God's message of judgment was addressed to the nation as a whole, it was to be acted upon by every individual in that nation. It is the same today: God not only wants all men to hear the gospel, He wants each one individually to heed and obey it so that they might be saved. Through Amos, God gave warning of impending judgment so that the people might have opportunity to repent. The people should have listened to God - He had the right to their hearing since He had redeemed them from slavery in Egypt. Sadly, history reveals that they did not listen, and that judgment fell.

> 3:2 You only have I known of all the families of the earth; therefore I will punish you for all your iniquities.

Israel's privileged position brought greater responsibility. When He brought them out of the land of Egypt, God made a covenant with them by which they became His own people. He had not done this for any other nation on earth. The word "known" denotes an intimate relationship, as between a husband and wife. God had taken Israel to Himself as a husband takes a wife to himself. Israel should have been only for God, she should have delighted herself in Him - but she had left her maker-husband to seek other gods, idols that she called her "lords". Having known the Lord, she turned away from Him - a far more serious sin than if she had never known God. Hers was not the sin of ignorance but of deliberate rebellion.

Christians are reminded of the seriousness of turning away from God after coming to know Him *(Hebrews 6: 4 - 6)*. It is our Christian responsibility, not to live as we like, but as He likes. Our relationship with God will not exclude us from His punishment for wrongs, as Peter reminds us, *"judgment begins at the house of God" (1 Peter 4:17)*.

> *3:3 Can two walk together, unless they are agreed? (NKJV™).*

God had brought Israel into a covenant relationship with Himself, but the fellowship and blessings that came through that covenant were conditional on obedience. Since the nation had rebelled against God, disobeyed His commands and rejected His covenant, their fellowship with God was broken.

The Prophet Defends His Office

> *3:4 Does a lion roar in the forest, when it has no prey? Does a young lion cry out from its den, if it has caught nothing?*

Just as a lion does not roar if it has no prey, so God does not speak without reason. God never wastes His words. Israel had sinned and God pronounced judgment through Amos. Israel, to its peril, had so far ignored these warnings. If they thought that God would speak without carrying out His words, they were very much mistaken.

> *3:5 Does a bird fall into a snare on the earth, when there is no trap for it? Does a snare spring up from the ground, when it has taken nothing?*

Disaster does not come by chance. It is God's doing. A bird is not caught in a net unless one is set for it by a hunter. God is the hunter and Israel the bird. The Assyrian army may be thought of as the net. It was not coincidence or bad luck, but Divine judgment that would bring the Assyrian invasion. The trap will not spring in vain. The little bird will be caught and killed. Israel will have no hope of escaping the judgment to come. History records that it came less than thirty years later.

> *3:6 Is a trumpet blown in a city, and the people are not afraid? Does disaster befall a city, unless the LORD has done it?*

It was generally true that if a trumpet was blown in a city, the people would fear, for they knew that it signalled the approach of a hostile enemy. Yet although God had sounded the warning trumpet by the lips of His prophets, the people remained unconcerned. They took no notice whatever of God's messengers. So when the warning trumpet actually sounded, it would be too late, for it would herald the approach of the Assyrian army, unstoppable, since they were sent by God, who remains directly and completely in control of the affairs of individuals and nations.

Daniel 4:17 "The Most High rules in the kingdom of men, Gives it to whomever He will, And sets over it the lowest of men." (NKJV™).

"Unexpectedly indeed calamity comes, and it is commonly ascribed to chance. But the prophet here reminds us that God stretches His net, in which men are caught, though they think that chance rules and observe not the hand of God. They are deceived, he says, for the bird foresees not the ensnaring prepared for him; but yet he falls not on the earth without the fowler; for nets weave not themselves by chance, but they are made by the industry of the man who catches birds. So also calamities happen not by chance, but proceed from the secret purposes of God." John Calvin (Cited by Beeley, 1969)

> *3:7 Surely the Lord GOD does nothing, without revealing his secret to his servants the prophets.*

God wills to reveal Himself to men, that they may know Him. Nothing God does is ever done in a corner. In His long-suffering, God gives all men opportunity to repent of their sin. This fact is demonstrated by the way that His judgments on Israel had been announced in advance, with many prophets sent to warn them of impending disaster. God even sent the prophet Jonah out of Israel to warn the heathen city of Nineveh - a foretaste of a coming day when His mercy would embrace all men through the gospel of His Son. Today, as then, God gives men time and opportunity to act on the warnings of future judgment given in the scripture and embrace pardon for sin through His Son Jesus Christ.

Not only unbelievers but believers who continue in their sin are first given warning before God acts to discipline and correct them. In Revelation 2:21 Christ informed the local church of His dealings with an immoral Christian woman, saying, "I gave her space to repent of her sexual immorality". This was not the space of silence, for God had spoken by His word to the individual concerned. But His warnings being unheeded, He was forced to act. As Israel had learned years before, men must heed what God does, even if they refuse to heed what He says.

> *3:8 The lion has roared; who will not fear? The Lord GOD has spoken; who can but prophesy?*

Any man who hears the approach of a lion should consider himself responsible to warn others and avert disaster. God had spoken of impending judgment and so Amos felt compelled to speak. The apostle Paul knew the same feeling. Knowing the truth of the gospel and having experienced the grace of God who had saved him from sin, he felt constrained to speak by the love of Christ *(2 Corinthians 5:14)*.

Since God was not willing for any to perish, Paul did not withhold the message of salvation from anyone.

We must again apply this to our present time. Christians are in possession of the truth. Unless we speak, souls will perish. There is no question as to whether God would have us speak. It is not a case of "maybe we ought to do a bit of evangelism". We are compelled by both a moral obligation and a Divine commission. God described the prophet Ezekiel as a watchman *(Ezekiel 3:17)*. The watchman was to look out for approaching enemies so that he might give prior warning to the people. Today, Christians are all watchmen, for since we know what is to come (the glory of the redeemed and the judgment of the wicked), God will hold us responsible for making it known *(Ezekiel 33:6)*.

A Remnant Will be Saved

> *3:9 Proclaim to the strongholds in Ashdod, and to the strongholds in the land of Egypt, and say, "Assemble yourselves on Mount Samaria, and see what great tumults are within it, and what oppressions are in its midst."*

The picture here is of a law court. God calls two witnesses to the stand, enemies of Israel. They are to observe the violence and oppression which was taking place in the nation, so that they would understand God's punishment on His people. God was going to demonstrate His justice on Israel in the sight of all nations and we may suppose that this was meant to serve as a warning to them.

> *3:10 They do not know how to do right, says the LORD, those who store up violence and robbery in their strongholds.*

God's people were so practised in doing evil that they had forgotten how to do right. It was not that they did not know God's word; it was that they had refused to listen and hardened their hearts until they became deaf to God and enslaved by their sin. All of us, before we came to know Jesus Christ as our Saviour were slaves of sin and unable to free ourselves, for only Jesus can break the power of sin in our lives *(John 8:36)*.

The people were living the life of luxury, yet their wealth had been obtained by unjust means, and through extortion and violence. As I write, the excesses of political leaders and business executives are once again in the headlines. The problem is an old one, and so is the answer - not merely social reform but a genuine repentance toward God resulting in social reform. The scripture gives a blessing for those who remember the poor, but God condemns those who are guilty of social and economic sins.

> *3:11 Therefore thus says the Lord GOD: An adversary shall surround the land, and strip you of your defense; and your strongholds shall be plundered.*

Because of their sin, God would bring an enemy to invade the land and lay siege to them (this meaning is better clarified in the NKJV™, which uses the phrase "sapping of strength" - it would be a prolonged war of attrition). The Assyrian army later did plunder and destroy the fortified towns of Israel just as Amos had predicted.

> *3:12 Thus says the LORD: As the shepherd rescues from the mouth of the lion two legs, or a piece of an ear, so shall the people of Israel who live in Samaria be rescued, with the corner of a couch and part of a bed.*

God promised that a remnant of the people would be spared - a remnant chosen by His grace for the continuance of the nation, because of the promises He had made. The illustration given indicates that a very small number would remain in Samaria. The Living Bible reads: *The Lord says, "A shepherd tried to rescue his sheep from a lion, but it was too late; he snatched from the lion's mouth two legs and a piece of ear. So it will be when the Israelites in Samaria are finally rescued--all they will have left is half a chair and a tattered pillow." Amos 3:12 (Living).*

> 3:13 Hear, and testify against the house of Jacob, says the Lord GOD, the God of hosts:

God is still figuratively speaking to the witnesses described in verse nine.

> 3:14 On the day I punish Israel for its transgressions, I will punish the altars of Bethel, and the horns of the altar shall be cut off and fall to the ground.

When God brings this calamity because of the peoples' sin, He will destroy the root of the nation's apostasy - the idolatrous altars at Bethel. By the "horns falling to the ground" we understand that God intended to completely remove the influence of pagan religion from among the people.

> 3:15 I will tear down the winter house as well as the summer house; and the houses of ivory shall perish, and the great houses shall come to an end, says the LORD.

Despite earlier warnings, the nation remained unconcerned, largely due to the fact that they were comfortable and well off financially. Their wealth had become their security, and the love of riches rather the love of God ruled their hearts. It was Jesus who said that no man can serve two masters *(Matthew 6:24)*. Not only would Israel have to learn that it could not serve both God and the calves at Bethel but also that it could not serve God and material wealth (mammon). Nor can we.

How relevant this is for Christians today, many of whom live in comparative luxury, and yet remain lukewarm in their love for God and unconcerned about the need of a world lost in sin. Material and financial security will be swept away in the day of God's judgment. All Israel had accumulated would be lost in a short space of time. This will always be the inevitable result.

Since none of us can take his wealth with him beyond the grave, we would be wiser, in the words of Christ, to *"lay up treasures in heaven" (Matthew 6:20).*

And I will destroy the beautiful homes of the wealthy--their winter mansions and their summer houses too--and demolish their ivory palaces. Amos 3:15 (Living)

Amos 4:1–13. Hypocritical Religion

Punishment for "Fat Cows"

4:1 Hear this word, you cows of Bashan who are on Mount Samaria, who oppress the poor, who crush the needy, who say to their husbands, "Bring something to drink!"

The prophet refers to the women of Samaria as "fat cows". Bashan was known as a fertile place where the cattle grazed well and became fat. These women lived in luxury and drove their husbands to provide for their self-indulgence in ways that oppressed the poor, whose rights were ignored and whose plight was never given a second thought.

A good wife can be a tower of strength to her husband, especially if he is in the service of the Lord - but a wife who thinks of her own interests above those of everyone else will be her husband's undoing. For example, Jezebel's influence over Ahab led him to evil actions for the furtherance of her selfish and evil ends. God will hold us all responsible not only for what we do, but for what we influence others to do *(see Mark 9.42)*.

God refers to these women as brute beasts since they live only to gratify their animal or sensual appetites, constantly indulging in strong drink and revelry *(2 Peter 2.12; Philippians 3.18–19)*.

4:2–3 The Lord GOD has sworn by his holiness: The time is surely coming upon you, when they shall take you away with hooks, even the last of you with fishhooks. Through breaches in the wall you shall leave, each one straight ahead; and you shall be flung out into Harmon, says the LORD.

On oath of His own immutable holiness, God decreed the punishment of these self-satisfied and callous women. Since they behaved like cattle they would, together with their children, be led away like cattle, pulled along with hooks in their mouths. This method was literally employed by their conquerors the Assyrians when they broke down the walls of the city and took the women and children captive as slaves, ending their days of ease and luxury.

You will be hauled from your beautiful homes and tossed out through the nearest breach in the wall. Amos 4:3 (Living)

Religious Pride and Hypocrisy

> *4:4–5 Come to Bethel--and transgress; to Gilgal--and multiply transgression; bring your sacrifices every morning, your tithes every three days; bring a thank offering of leavened bread, and proclaim freewill offerings, publish them; for so you love to do, O people of Israel! says the Lord GOD.*

Israel's hypocrisy increased their guilt. Whilst living in sin and self-indulgence they continued to worship God, albeit in an idolatrous manner. They worshipped the idols (who were meant, initially, to represent God Himself) at Bethel and Gilgal, in breach of the second commandment *(Exodus 20:4–5)*.

As Christians, we too should be aware of the dangers of approaching God in hypocrisy. When we come to the communion service knowing that we have sin in our lives which we have neither confessed nor forsaken, we are acting as these hypocrites did and will be judged by God *(1 Corinthians 11:27–32)*.

The women of Israel made much of their daily sacrifices to God, of their bringing tithes and making thank offerings. They boasted about it as if their religion made them superior to others. Christ warned his followers of the danger of this (see Matthew 6:1–5 & Matthew 6:16–18). Christians may fall into the trap of portraying themselves as superior - but such an attitude will never win the unconverted. Only as we show respect to all people can we win them for Christ *(1 Peter 3:15–16)*.

Like the Pharisees in Jesus' time, the women of Israel gave an outward impression of being righteous, whilst corruption was in their heart (Matthew 23:27–28). They loved their religious practices and would not neglect them for anything, but they did not love God, or the poor.

God is never *impressed* by our singing, praying, preaching or giving. Yet He is *pleased* when the motivation for all we do is love for Him.

God's Dealings to Israel to Repentance

> *4:6 I gave you cleanness of teeth in all your cities, and lack of bread in all your places, yet you did not return to me, says the LORD.*

God had chastened His people in various ways in order to bring them back to Himself, and laments that even so they had not repented. Firstly, He had sent famine to the land. Their cleanness of teeth (we would say, "empty stomachs") was due to the lack of bread.

> *4:7–8 And I also withheld the rain from you when there were still three months to the harvest; I would send rain on one city, and send no rain on another city; one field would be rained upon, and the field on which it did not rain withered; so two or three towns wandered to one town to drink water, and were not satisfied; yet you did not return to me, says the LORD.*

Next came drought. The rains which were needed to ripen the harvest never came. As if to demonstrate His control over these events, God caused it to rain in one part of the country but not another so that people had to go in search of water to drink. But even then there was not sufficient for all.

> *4:9 I struck you with blight and mildew; I laid waste your gardens and your vineyards; the locust devoured your fig trees and your olive trees; yet you did not return to me, says the LORD.*

Crops were destroyed by disease and fruits were ruined by insects, yet the people did not repent and return to God.

> *4:10 I sent among you a pestilence after the manner of Egypt; I killed your young men with the sword; I carried away your horses; and I made the stench of your camp go up into your nostrils; yet you did not return to me, says the LORD.*

The diseases and plagues which came one after another on man and beast should have been enough to warn the Israelites that their sin and disobedience were not being overlooked, but even the obvious similarity to what God had done to the Egyptians, and which He was now forced to do to them, was not enough to bring them to repentance. Enemy troops had made forays into Israel's territory and destroyed men and captured horses, leaving the land devastated, but the people had not returned to God.

> *4:11 I overthrew some of you, as when God overthrew Sodom and Gomorrah, and you were like a brand snatched from the fire; yet you did not return to me, says the LORD.*

It is clear from this verse that some terrible disaster had occurred to completely destroy whole cities in Israel in a way reminiscent of what happened to Sodom. Then, the cities of Sodom and Gomorrah were destroyed by fire out of heaven. Here, however, it is more likely that an earthquake had caused the disaster, since such an earthquake is referred to in chapter one. Although the whole nation deserved punishment, only some cities were destroyed, an act of mercy whereby God kept the remainder of the nation alive and gave them a further opportunity to repent. "Brands from the burning" are those who are saved from destruction by God's mercy *(Jude 1:23 & Zechariah 3:2).*

Final Judgment is Inevitable

> *4:12 Therefore thus I will do to you, O Israel; because I will do this to you, prepare to meet your God, O Israel!*

Since, despite all these measured judgments, intended as they were to bring the nation to repentance, the nation had not repented, they must now suffer the consequences of their rebellion. The same is applies to the impenitent today, if we will not meet with God in mercy then we must meet with Him in judgment and it is a fearful thing to fall into the hands of the Living God. It is eternal punishment that the prophet has in mind when he says, *"prepare to meet your God."*

> *4:13 For lo, the one who forms the mountains, creates the wind, reveals his thoughts to mortals, makes the morning darkness, and treads on the heights of the earth--the LORD, the God of hosts, is his name!*

In this beautiful poem of praise, the qualifications of the One who is to be their Judge are set before the children of Israel. The Creator of all things is terrible in might and majesty, there is no limit to His power.

Hence He should be obeyed, loved and served. He alone is able to judge men righteously for He not only knows their actions but also the thoughts and motives of their hearts. Since He is exalted far above all, man's resistance of Him may be seen for what it is: both puny and futile.

Amos 5:1-27. *A Lament for the Nation*

In this chapter, God reveals His people's sin and warns them of its consequences, before making known the remedy and revealing the blessings which would come as a result of applying it.

A Lament for the Nation

> *5:1–2 Hear this word that I take up over you in lamentation, O house of Israel: Fallen, no more to rise, is maiden Israel; forsaken on her land, with no one to raise her up.*

Having spoken in chapter four of the judgment soon to come on the land, God proceeds to take up a lament. A lament was a song of mourning - a funeral dirge for someone who had died. Who was dead? It was the nation of Israel, once God's own peculiar treasure, intended to be His alone (as a "maiden" or "virgin daughter" should keep herself for her husband alone). Yet Israel had gone after other gods and so God would remove His protection from her that she might be utterly destroyed and never rise again. Since it was God Himself who handed her over to her enemies, who could help her? Being forsaken by her Maker, no one could raise her up.

"No one to raise her up" should be understood in context. It did not mean the complete annihilation of all the people, as the next verse clearly shows. Neither did it mean that Israel would never be a nation again. It paints, however, a vivid picture of the absolute devastation that would come to the nation as a result of war with Assyria. The nation of that time would never recover from this war.

> *5:3 For thus says the Lord GOD: The city that marched out a thousand shall have a hundred left, and that which marched out a hundred shall have ten left.*

The LORD predicts that only a tenth of the present population would survive the coming holocaust.

Through this lament we see that the judgment of God is always accompanied by deep sorrow. God takes no pleasure in the death of the wicked, and is not willing for any to perish. He would have all to be saved by responding in repentance and faith to His word. But although God had done all in His power to avoid this tragedy, but the nation was still not willing to repent (*compare Luke 19:41–44*).

> 5:4 For thus says the LORD to the house of Israel: Seek me and live;

At the same time that God spoke to warn Israel of impending judgment, He gave them another opportunity to repent. The root of all Israel's' sin was that she had forsaken God. The only remedy therefore was to repent and seek God (*Isaiah 55:6–7*). The Bible promises eternal life to those who seek God (*Romans 2:7*) since to know God is to have eternal life (*John 17:3*). Before we can know God we must first seek Him and if we do so by searching His word with honest hearts we shall discover first of all that we are sinners, separated from Him by our wicked deeds and unable for this reason to enter heaven. Then we shall find that Christ died for our sins according to the Scriptures and that He rose from the dead on the third day according to the Scriptures. We shall learn that all who believe in the Lord Jesus Christ receive eternal life. Only once we have received Christ as our Saviour can we truly say that we know God (or as Paul puts it in Galatians 4:9 - we are "known to God"), because we have become His children (*John 1:12*). Thereafter, we are to continue to seek God as the source and satisfaction of our lives.

Seek God in Truth

> *5:5 but do not seek Bethel, and do not enter into Gilgal or cross over to Beer-sheba; for Gilgal shall surely go into exile, and Bethel shall come to nothing.*

Having urged the people to seek God, the prophet warns them not to seek Him at the centres of idolatrous worship. God has already expressed His judgment on these places. Perhaps a play on words is intended here. Gilgal means "rolled away" and it shall be rolled away - into captivity in Assyria and so will Bethel (the house of God) become "nothing" or "Beth Aven" (lit. the house of emptiness, that is, desolate).

The warning is applicable today. Those who seek for God must look for Him in the right place. Our worship of God must be according to the revealed truth of His Word. (*John 4:24*). Sadly, many today are turning to crystals, horoscopes, the occult, Feng Shui, etc. because they are seeking for spiritual reality, truth and life. Unfortunately, they shall find neither life nor reality in any of these things, but only death, for all these routes lead to eternal damnation. Only Jesus Christ is the Way, the Truth and the Life, and only through Him can we know God (*John 14:6*).

> *5:6 Seek the LORD and live, or he will break out against the house of Joseph like fire, and it will devour Bethel, with no one to quench it.*

We must seek the Lord Himself if we are to enjoy eternal, spiritual and abundant life (*John 10:10*). Amos warned Israel that if she failed to do so then God's judgment would destroy the nation, rather like fire destroys the chaff which is burned after harvest because it is useless. The phrase *"with no one to quench it"* reveals that the wrath of God cannot be turned away from those who are impenitent. If God had found even ten penitent souls in Bethel, then He may have mitigated the disaster for the sake of those ten, *(see Genesis 18:20 - 32)* but there was no one. In the New Testament, Jesus warned the impenitent of eternal judgment. In hell, Jesus said, the fire would never be put out, meaning that the punishment of the lost soul would never end *(Mark 9:44).*

> *5:7 Ah, you that turn justice to wormwood, and bring righteousness to the ground!*

As terrible as God's judgments are, they are always right and fair. The people of Israel, however, had abandoned fairness so that justice did not prevail in their law courts. In vivid language Amos describes the nation's justice as being dead and buried (*"to the ground"*, that is, buried in the ground). The weak or poor were oppressed by the rich and influential. Someone has paraphrased the verse, *"Justice was turned in to a bitter pill. Righteousness and fair play became meaningless fictions." (anonymous quote, cited by Beeley).*

Today, whenever courts deny justice or place the rights of an offender above the rights of the victim; or whenever governments and courts overlook the commandments of God in favour of humanist regulations, misleadingly called "human rights" (*see Matthew 15:9*) we ought not be surprised to learn that the same judgment of eternal fire (mentioned in verse 6) is reserved for them.

> *5:8 The one who made the Pleiades and Orion, and turns deep darkness into the morning, and darkens the day into night, who calls for the waters of the sea, and pours them out on the surface of the earth, the LORD is his name,*

The people who had sunk to the worship of the so called "star deities" are called upon to seek the One who made the stars. How different God is to idols! He is the Lord of Creation, bringing light and darkness and rain. He had made himself known to Israel by His name "the LORD", the self-existent and sovereign God. *(See also chapter 9 verse 6).*

> *5:9 who makes destruction flash out against the strong, so that destruction comes upon the fortress.*

As God is sovereign in creation so He is also in the affairs of men. It is not the might of armies but God who decides the outcome of a battle and so directs the course of history. He gives strength to the weak and enables them to destroy their oppressors. God would demonstrate that it is He, not the star deities, who directs the steps of men, as Beeley says *"The heathen thought of the stars directing the course of history, but it is He (God) who made the stars who does so."*

> *5:10 They hate the one who reproves in the gate, and they abhor the one who speaks the truth.*

Those who love evil live in darkness and hate the light. Whatever reproves and convinces of sin is light (*Ephesians 5:13*). That is why the Israelites, who loved sin, hated all who spoke out against it. It was for the very same reason that they hated, rejected and crucified the Lord Jesus Christ (*John 7:7*).

> *5:11 Therefore because you trample on the poor and take from them levies of grain, you have built houses of hewn stone, but you shall not live in them; you have planted pleasant vineyards, but you shall not drink their wine.*

The rich were oppressing the poor by an unfair system of taxation. The poor were burdened with taxes whilst the rich feathered their own nests. For this reason, God would snatch away the ill-gotten gains of the rich. The houses they had built and the vineyards they had bought with the proceeds of their extortion would no longer be theirs to occupy or enjoy.

Today, any nation that ignores the Divine principles of social justice will find that its prosperity will only be short lived.

> *5:12 For I know how many are your transgressions, and how great are your sins--you who afflict the righteous, who take a bribe, and push aside the needy in the gate.*

Those who dwell in darkness like to think that God cannot see them, and that He is not aware of their evil deeds. But God sees and knows all things (*Psalm 94:7–9*). He saw the many ways in which Israel had broken His laws and how very great their guilt was ("your mighty sins"). The just and the poor were their favourite targets, probably because they offered no retaliation. Officials accepted bribes to pervert the course of justice, with the highest bidder getting the result they wanted in a court case. Note: The gate of the town/city was where the elders (magistrates) gathered during the day - it served as a court where any one could bring a dispute to be settled.

> *5:13 Therefore the prudent will keep silent in such a time; for it is an evil time.*

Those who were wise kept silent at such a time - since they knew that whatever they said would not alter the situation but would only serve to make themselves a target. It does not always seem right to stay silent about moral issues, but here the Lord Himself declares that there are times when it is prudent.

A Promise for the Repentant

> *5:14–15 Seek good and not evil, that you may live; and so the LORD, the God of hosts, will be with you, just as you have said. Hate evil and love good, and establish justice in the gate; it may be that the LORD, the God of hosts, will be gracious to the remnant of Joseph.*

God always warns mankind of His judgments so that man has time to take action and repent. If the people chose God's way, by seeking good not evil, and giving justice in their law courts then:

i. God would be with them as a nation as they were vainly boasting that He was.

ii. they would live. (In context, this promise is to the whole nation, but the principle applies to each individual).

iii. Judgment would be avoided and the Lord would be gracious to those who were left in Israel. (The word "Joseph" was sometimes used as a reference to the northern kingdom of Israel).

God bestows blessings on repentant hearts, but that does imply that God's blessings are earned, for as Beeley says *"forgiveness is always a privilege not a right...men are commanded to repent - this is their duty as moral creatures - but even then forgiveness is still an act of grace. Men are forgiven when they repent, not because they repent."*

The Day of the Lord

> *5:16 Therefore thus says the LORD, the God of hosts, the Lord: In all the squares there shall be wailing; and in all the streets*

> they shall say, "Alas! alas!" They shall call the farmers to mourning, and those skilled in lamentation, to wailing;

God had given His promise to bless and forgive the repentant, but since the people adamantly refused to repent, the rebellion of the nation would bring swift judgment - the invasion of the Assyrian army would bring death, destruction and mourning to the whole land.

> 5:17 in all the vineyards there shall be wailing, for I will pass through the midst of you, says the LORD.

These shattering events would not happen by chance. God says "I will pass through you". The Assyrians were merely God's weapon, His instrument of punishment, by which He would judge Israel. The phrase "pass through" stands in deliberate contrast with the more familiar "pass over". On the night that the death angel brought judgment to the Egyptians, Israel was spared, for God passed over them. But now, God would pass through them, bringing destruction and grief at the hands of the Assyrian army. Since vineyards are symbols of fruitfulness and joy, their literal destruction is also a symbol of the nation's joy being turned into grief.

> 5:18 Alas for you who desire the day of the LORD! Why do you want the day of the LORD? It is darkness, not light;

The people had deceived themselves, misunderstanding what was meant by the idea of, "The Day of the Lord". Many prophets had spoken of it. The people knew that it would be a day when God Himself would visit them. The term can in fact be used to mean any occasion when God will act, reveal Himself and meet in person with His people. Israel welcomed this. Since they were the chosen people of God, the descendants of Abraham, they presumed that when God visited them it would be to bless, prosper them and to rescue them from their enemies.

God makes clear, however, that when He does visit them, it will be to enter into judgment with them. Although they were not concerned about their sin, God was. He would teach His covenant people that He is holy and too pure to look at sin. Whilst it is true that God takes no pleasure in the death of the wicked, it is also true that God must and will punish the ungodly (*Ezekiel 33:11; Jude 1:15; 2 Peter 2:9*).

> *5:19 as if someone fled from a lion, and was met by a bear; or went into the house and rested a hand against the wall, and was bitten by a snake.*

The prophet vividly describes God meeting with Israel in fierce wrath. There would be no escape. The Divine sentence had been pronounced: that day would spell doom for unrepentant Israel.

> *5:20 Is not the day of the LORD darkness, not light, and gloom with no brightness in it?*

Ray Beeley says, *"Darkness here is used as a symbol for terror and doom. There will be no shadow of hope for the ungodly in that day."* The same may be said concerning the day when God will judge those who have not received His Son the Lord Jesus Christ as their Saviour. It will be a day of darkness and no light. It will be a day of judgment and no mercy. It will be the day when those who have rejected Christ will enter damnation eternally with no hope of ever escaping *(Revelation 14:9–11; Mark 9:44)*.

Sincerity in Worship

> *5:21 I hate, I despise your festivals, and I take no delight in your solemn assemblies.*

If there is one thing that God hates more than anything else, it is hypocrisy. The people of Israel were not living in a way that honoured the Lord: they had broken His laws, treated others unfairly and oppressed the poor and yet they turned up for worship at the "House of God". They observed solemn feast days, but their religious meetings were offensive to God.

> *5:22 Even though you offer me your burnt offerings and grain offerings, I will not accept them; and the offerings of well-being of your fatted animals I will not look upon.*

Even when the people made offerings and sacrifices to God, they were not accepted, for their hearts, motives and lives were not right in His sight.

> *5:23 Take away from me the noise of your songs; I will not listen to the melody of your harps.*

Their singing and playing instruments of praise and worship did not gain them an audience in heaven either - God could not even bear to hear it. It was not acceptable to Him, He would rather they shut up *(Malachi 1:10)*.

As Christians we would do well to bear in mind what God said to His ancient people. It is possible to come to church and go through the motions of singing and praising God without our worship coming from a pure heart that is wholly devoted to the Lord and willing to obey Him. The hypocrisy of religious service without sincerity and obedience is what Christ denounced the Pharisees for *(Matthew 15:7–9)*.

> *5:24 But let justice roll down like waters, and righteousness like an ever-flowing stream.*

Israel made the mistake of thinking they could worship God without living by His righteous laws. We too must beware of thinking we can ignore God's standards *(Romans 6:1–2)*. God wants our religion to be expressed in right relationships and right conduct. Jesus said that those who worship God must worship Him in Spirit and truth. The work of the Spirit is to produce the life of Christ in us, and Jesus always obeyed and did the will of His Father. In this way, righteousness is like an ever-flowing stream, since, *"Those who do the will of God, live forever" (1 John 2:17).*

The Sin of Idolatry

> *5:25–27 Did you bring to me sacrifices and offerings the forty years in the wilderness, O house of Israel? You shall take up Sakkuth your king, and Kaiwan your star-god, your images, which you made for yourselves; therefore I will take you into exile beyond Damascus, says the LORD, whose name is the God of hosts.*

To make matters far worse, whilst Israel professed to be worshipping God, they are actually bowing down to idols. This was perhaps the most serious sin of all, since it was deliberate rejection of the Lord. Mixing the worship of God with that of idols was in direct disobedience to the Second Commandment *(Exodus 20:4–5)*.

Today, Christians must be careful not to mix what is holy with what is unholy *(1 Corinthians 10:21)*. To have "one foot in the world and another foot in the church" is to be in a precarious position indeed. For all its evil deeds the world is to be judged, and so the commandment of God to His people today is: *"Therefore come out from them, and be separate from them, says the Lord, and touch nothing unclean; then I will welcome you (2 Corinthians 6:17).*

During their forty years of desert wanderings, Israel had worshipped the idols named here, fashioned by their own hands in honour of the pagan star deities and tragically the heart of the nation had not changed. "The God of hosts" had made the stars and it was He who brought Israel out of Egypt and made them a nation. He alone had the right to their devotion and worship. Because of their unfaithfulness, God would punish the nation by sending them far away. They would be taken and resettled by the Assyrians "beyond Damascus", that is further afield than Damascus (which itself was 130 miles north of Jerusalem).

Amos 6:1–14. Warning to the Unconcerned

A Warning to the Unconcerned

6:1 Alas for those who are at ease in Zion, and for those who feel secure on Mount Samaria, the notables of the first of the nations, to whom the house of Israel resorts!

Amos brought a message of warning to those who were:

a) unconcerned. Those in government did not care about the moral and spiritual state of the nation, nor their own moral bankruptcy. It is foolish and dangerous to be careless about one's spiritual condition, especially with regard to one's eternal salvation. *(Hebrews 2:3; Luke 12:16–21)*.

b) inactive. Those who are "at ease" are doing nothing. They fail to fulfil their responsibility to God and men. If the first point was about being careless about the condition of our own souls, the second is about being careless for the souls of others. In Christ's parable, the unfaithful servant was judged for "doing nothing" *(Matthew 25:14–30)*. Let us be careful to fulfil our responsibilities to Christ, to His Church and to the unconverted.

c) comfortable. Their conscience was undisturbed. To them, sin was not to be loathed, it was something to do when you wanted to. Spurgeon says, *"Their convictions are superficial...there is no subsoil ploughing, no turning up and breaking of the clods...no revelation of themselves to themselves." (Cited by Beeley)*.

When threatened with invasion, the people did not rest their confidence on God, but in the natural situation of Samaria, which being in the mountains seemed to offer a measure of protection and safety. Their confidence was misplaced. Today, many put their confidence in their own goodness or religious observance as the means of making them right with God, whereas Paul writes, *"we have no confidence in the flesh"* (Philippians 1:3). It is Christ alone who can save us.

Israel saw themselves as the greatest of nations and made this their boast. They had forgotten that it was God who had brought them out of Egypt to make them a nation and had given them the land they now occupied.

> *6:2 Cross over to Calneh, and see; from there go to Hamath the great; then go down to Gath of the Philistines. Are you better than these kingdoms? Or is your territory greater than their territory,*

The towns mentioned were once larger and more powerful than Samaria. Yet they had been destroyed by the Assyrian army. In the same way, Israel would not escape, since her sins were just as serious as those of the other nations.

> *6:3 O you that put far away the evil day, and bring near a reign of violence?*

Because the people had not experienced God's punishment for their sin immediately, they thought it would never come at all *(Ecclesiastes 8:11)*. They continued unconcerned in their sin, but their obstinate attitude simply hastened the day when God would punish them.

Pride and Selfish Indulgence

> *6:4–5 6 Alas for those who lie on beds of ivory, and lounge on their couches, and eat lambs from the flock, and calves from the stall; who sing idle songs to the sound of the harp, and like*

David improvise on instruments of music; who drink wine from bowls, and anoint themselves with the finest oils, but are not grieved over the ruin of Joseph!

Amos describes the luxury in which the people lived. The well-known wealthy business men remained idle, sparing themselves no luxury as they paid others next to nothing to do their work for them. The rich had all they wanted for themselves (note their rich diet) but did not once consider giving anything to the poor among God's people.

Selfishness can be a problem in the Christian life, too. Perhaps we should ask ourselves whether we are giving our best to the Lord, or taking the best for ourselves and leaving God the left overs.

With time on their hands, they fancied themselves to be good musicians like David and invented instruments as he did. Yet David had devoted his talent to the service of God and for worship. They used their (lesser) talents for their own entertainment. How we use the gifts that God has given us is an important question. Is it for ourselves or for Him? God will hold us all accountable for what we do with our time, money and talents. Even the best Christian "worship songs" can be no better than "idle singing" if sung for our own pleasure or entertainment rather than for God's glory.

These revellers loved to party. Their drinking habits were excessive. Instead of cups they used bowls. The Living Bible translates the start of verse 6 as, *"You drink wine by the bucketful."* Drink flowed freely in their parties.

The gospel writers record how a woman poured costly perfume on Jesus *(Mark 14:3)*. In this chapter we see the women spending large sums to pour perfume on themselves. The best of the sheep and cattle should have been offered to God. Instead, they were eaten, a brazen insult to Jehovah *(Malachi 1:6–8)*.

All of this demonstrated that they had no concern for their own spiritual condition, that of the nation, nor for the hardships faced daily by their fellow countrymen. They were callous, like Joseph's brothers who ate a meal as he cried to them from the pit. How different to the Lord Jesus Christ who wept over the city of Jerusalem because of the moral and spiritual bankruptcy of the people, and for what would happen to them subsequent to their rejection of Him *(Luke 19:41–44)*.

Ray Beeley asks, *"How much self-indulgence am I prepared to allow myself? Remember how the Son, 'pleased not Himself.'"* *(see John 6:38; Romans 15:3; Hebrews 5:8)*.

> *6:7 Therefore they shall now be the first to go into exile, and the revelry of the loungers shall pass away.*

These revellers would be the very first casualties of the war - taken captive by the enemy. In this way, God says, He will cause their revelry to cease.

> *6:8 The Lord GOD has sworn by himself (says the LORD, the God of hosts): I abhor the pride of Jacob and hate his strongholds; and I will deliver up the city and all that is in it.*

God hated the pride and false glory of Israel. What they thought was glory to them - their wealth, influence, fame and importance - was in His eyes shameful. God was the true glory of the nation and they should have trusted in Him. In our modern day, we should fear for the security of any nation that boasts in its own glories, whether financial, cultural or military - but does not place its hope in God. Without Him, the greatest boast of any man or nation is empty. Because Israel trusted themselves and not God, they would be handed over to their enemies.

The Severity of the Coming Judgment

> *6:9 If ten people remain in one house, they shall die.*

Amos again warns of the severity of the coming judgment. Even the survivors of the Assyrian attack would later die, probably of disease.

> *6:10 And if a relative, one who burns the dead, shall take up the body to bring it out of the house, and shall say to someone in the innermost parts of the house, "Is anyone else with you?" the answer will come, "No." Then the relative shall say, "Hush! We must not mention the name of the LORD."*

If any relative were still alive, he would be responsible to cremate the dead bodies, the usual practice of burial being impractical due to the large numbers of dead. At that time men would be unwilling to even mention the name of the Lord, most probably because they feared to anger Him further. There is no doubt that they recognised that the hand of the Lord was in the judgment which had fallen upon them. What is regrettable is that they did not wish to acknowledge God, confess their sin and pray for His pardon.

> *6:11 See, the LORD commands, and the great house shall be shattered to bits, and the little house to pieces.*

There would be no respect of wealth or rank in the coming judgment. The whole nation would be affected and great and small alike would suffer. "Break into bits" means to leave gaps or breaches in the building and may refer not only to structural damage but also to the gaps left in families by death, "house" denoting household or family.

> 6:12 Do horses run on rocks? Does one plow the sea with oxen? But you have turned justice into poison and the fruit of righteousness into wormwood--

Would you expect a horse to run over rocks without being injured? Could you plough rocks with oxen? No, it is not sensible. Nor is it sensible for Israel to expect anything other than the judgment of God, since they had made the legal system a bitter poison through bias and unfairness so that the courts were corrupt and there was no justice in the land.

> 6:13 you who rejoice in Lo-debar, who say, "Have we not by our own strength taken Karnaim for ourselves?"

Israel was puffed up because of its recent military successes at the places mentioned. With such confidence in their own strength they thought themselves invincible. But salvation and victory come only from the Lord.

Today, we would do well to remember this warning. Only the Lord is able to save us from sin, leaving us with nothing to boast about (Ephesians 2:9; 1 Corinthians 1:29; Romans 3:27; Galatians 6.14).

> 6:14 Indeed, I am raising up against you a nation, O house of Israel, says the LORD, the God of hosts, and they shall oppress you from Lebo-hamath to the Wadi Arabah.

God would raise up the Assyrians to punish Israel, *"from the entrance of Hamath to the Valley of the Arabah"*, that is, the whole nation. In Great Britain we might say, "from Lands' End to John O' Groats".

Amos 7:1–17. Intercession and Opposition

Intercession for Israel

At the beginning of the chapter, Amos sees a series of three visions about God's judgment on the land of Israel. Each of the first two visions prompt Amos to pray to God on behalf of the nation. God relents as a result of the intercessory prayer of the prophet.

The Vision of Locusts

> *7:1 This is what the Lord GOD showed me: he was forming locusts at the time the latter growth began to sprout (it was the latter growth after the king's mowings).*

In the first vision, the Lord had determined to send swarms of locusts at the time when the food crop was to be harvested - after fodder had been cut for the king's animals.

> *7:2–3 When they had finished eating the grass of the land, I said, "O Lord GOD, forgive, I beg you! How can Jacob stand? He is so small!" The LORD relented concerning this; "It shall not be," said the LORD.*

The locusts ate every green thing, leaving no food for men or animals. Amos begs God to forgive the nation, for due to its weakness and small size it could not bear such a disaster. Such an event would utterly ruin the nation. In reply, the Lord relents. "It shall not be," He says.

The Vision of a Destroying Fire

> *7:4 This is what the Lord GOD showed me: the Lord GOD was calling for a shower of fire, and it devoured the great deep and was eating up the land.*

In the second vision, fire was sent out of heaven from God which burned up the sea and land. This would have devoured every living thing and Amos cries out for God to relent.

> 7:5–6 Then I said, "O Lord GOD, cease, I beg you! How can Jacob stand? He is so small!" The LORD relented concerning this; "This also shall not be," said the Lord GOD.

Again, through the intervention of the prophet, God relents and declares that this judgment also, "shall not be."

The Vision of the Plumb Line

> 7:7–8 This is what he showed me: the Lord was standing beside a wall built with a plumb line, with a plumb line in his hand. And the LORD said to me, "Amos, what do you see?" And I said, "A plumb line." Then the Lord said, "See, I am setting a plumb line in the midst of my people Israel; I will never again pass them by;

The vision suggests that although the wall had been built straight according to the plumb line, it was no longer straight. The builder would need to pull it down and start again.

God had made Israel a nation when He brought them out of Egypt, and had given them His own laws to live by. Rather than in the indiscriminate way described in the first two visions, God would judge them according to their privilege. The fact that they had received through the law the revelation of God made them more responsible than they otherwise would have been. Since they had broken His law and not repented they could no longer be spared. They were no longer upright. God's standard, however, represented by the plumb line, had not changed, and His judgment, like His standard, would be right and fair.

> 7:9 the high places of Isaac shall be made desolate, and the sanctuaries of Israel shall be laid waste, and I will rise against the house of Jeroboam with the sword."

Israel's pagan shrines would be destroyed and the worshippers slaughtered. Since it was Jeroboam the First who had introduced idolatry to the nation, all those who worshipped idols were considered his spiritual children *("the house of Jeroboam")* and would share in his judgment.

Opposition to the Word of God

Amaziah was a priest at Bethel where one of the golden calves was worshipped. As such, he was not a Levite appointed by God, but was appointed according to the command of Jeroboam the First. He had no right to the office of teaching God's people and was unable to lead them in God's ways. He raised a persecution against Amos simply because he was preaching the truth. It is because people love darkness rather than light that they react violently when they hear the truth.

> 7:10–11 Then Amaziah, the priest of Bethel, sent to King Jeroboam of Israel, saying, "Amos has conspired against you in the very center of the house of Israel; the land is not able to bear all his words. For thus Amos has said, 'Jeroboam shall die by the sword, and Israel must go into exile away from his land.'"

Amaziah wrote to the king, accusing Amos of treason because he had prophesied of the king's death. This accusation was false, because Amos had not referred to Jeroboam personally, but to his household, for as far as we know, Jeroboam did not die at the hands of the Assyrians. Amaziah correctly recounts details of Amos' prophecy concerning the captivity of Israel. Such a message, predicting defeat at the hands of their enemies, would not have been popular, and Amos was accused of stirring up civil unrest among the people "the land is not able to bear all his words."

Amos Threatened

> *7:12 And Amaziah said to Amos, "O seer, go, flee away to the land of Judah, earn your bread there, and prophesy there;*

Amaziah tries to intimidate Amos by telling him to run for his life before the king gets his letter. He advises him to go to Judah, where he could make a better living from prophesying. In saying this, Amaziah not only charges Amos with being a false prophet, but with having a wrong motive, that he only prophesies for financial gain. It should be remembered that Israel was at war with Judah at this time, *(2 Kings 14:28)* and Amaziah may have regarded Amos as an impostor hired by the king of Judah.

> *7:13 but never again prophesy at Bethel, for it is the king's sanctuary, and it is a temple of the kingdom."*

Although the priest threatened Amos with the authority of the king, Amos was sent by a greater authority than any king. It was true to say that Bethel is where the king worshipped, but it was not the place that God had ordained - for that was in Jerusalem- nor was it God who was worshipped at Bethel, but an image of God, which was outlawed by the second commandment *(Exodus 20:4–5).*

Amos knew that Amaziah was claiming for the king an authority that he did not have, just as Peter told the Sanhedrin *(Acts 4:19).*

Amos Defends His Ministry

> *7:14–15 Then Amos answered Amaziah, "I am no prophet, nor a prophet's son; but I am a herdsman, and a dresser of sycamore*

> trees, and the LORD took me from following the flock, and the LORD said to me, 'Go, prophesy to my people Israel.'

Amos, like Paul many years later, gives his own testimony in support for his preaching. He had not been brought up or trained as a prophet in some religious institution. He had been a farmer. It was not man but God who had revealed Himself to Amos and had sent him to preach to Israel. This is similar to the claim made by Paul in Galatians 1:1 *"Paul, an apostle (not from men nor through man, but through Jesus Christ and God the Father who raised Him from the dead)"* (NKJV™). The lack of a college or seminary training should never hold back the man or woman of God from fulfilling their Divine calling. It is the Lord Himself who sends His messengers forth with the gospel *(Romans 10:15; Acts 13:1 - 4)*.

We are all able to bear witness to the Lord. He has chosen and sent us to do this important work. As with Amos, our faithful witness to the Lord Jesus Christ may bring us persecution, perhaps from high quarters. But like Amos, we are enabled to stand for the truth, since like him we have been called and have a living experience of Jesus Christ *(Galatians 1:11–12)*.

It was as Amos was working as a herdsman, finding fodder for his cattle, that God called him. This is so often the case - it has been in our own experience. God breaks into lives and calls people when they are about the normal, daily business of living (see the call of Matthew in *Luke 5:27–28*; of Peter, James and John in *Mark 1:16–18*; and of Saul in his destructive business *Acts 9:1–5*).

It was in school as a boy that a friend witnessed to me about Jesus Christ. This is the usual way that someone is reached for Christ - in the ordinary pattern of life. That is why we must be where the Lord wants us, and be ready to "give an answer to anyone who asks us for the reason of the hope that we have" *(1 Peter 3:15* NKJV™*)*.

Amos Stands for the Truth

> *7:16 Now therefore hear the word of the LORD. You say, 'Do not prophesy against Israel, and do not preach against the house of Isaac.'*

In direct contradiction to God's command, Amaziah tells Amos NOT to prophesy. This is what the Sanhedrin told Peter and John in *Acts 4:18–20*. But like the apostles, Amos stood firmly for the truth. As he had said in chapter three, *"A lion has roared! Who will not fear? The Lord GOD has spoken! Who can but prophesy?" (Amos 3:8)*

Amaziah's Punishment

> *7:17 Therefore thus says the LORD: 'Your wife shall become a prostitute in the city, and your sons and your daughters shall fall by the sword, and your land shall be parceled out by line; you yourself shall die in an unclean land, and Israel shall surely go into exile away from its land.'*

There is no evading punishment for those who despise the word of the Lord. Because of his opposition to the word of God, Amaziah was to bring judgment on himself. He would be taken as a prisoner and exiled with Israel to Assyria, where he would die. His wife would be used as a prostitute, which may imply either that she would be raped by the invading soldiers, or that after Amaziah's exile, she would turn to prostitution as the only means of keeping herself alive. His children would all die at the hands of the invaders.

Amos 8:1-14. The Basket of Ripe Summer Fruit

A Basket of Ripe Ripe Summer Fruit

> 8:1 This is what the Lord GOD showed me--a basket of summer fruit.

In his vision, Amos saw a basket of ripe fruit, denoting that the time for harvest had come. God explains to Amos that the time for His judgment on Israel had come. They were ripe for judgment, since they had not heeded the warnings of the prophets. As a nation Israel had come to its end. This does not mean that every individual Jew would be wiped out, but that the nation would cease to be. It would not exist again until 1948.

> 8:2 He said, "Amos, what do you see?" And I said, "A basket of summer fruit." Then the LORD said to me, "The end has come upon my people Israel; I will never again pass them by.

God could no longer overlook the sin of His people. He would give them no further opportunity to repent. A farmer knows that he must act as soon as the crop is ripe *(see Revelation 14:14–19).*

At the end of the age, the Lord Jesus will gather his own (believers) safely to his barn (which is His presence - heaven). The ungodly, who are ripe for judgment are reaped and cast into the winepress of God, signifying eternal punishment *(Luke 3:17).*

> 8:3 And the songs of the temple Shall be wailing in that day," Says the Lord God-- "Many dead bodies everywhere, They shall be thrown out in silence." (NKJV™)

God was to put an end to the mirth of His disobedient people. As they caroused in the idol temples, their songs would be changed to cries and wails as the Assyrian army attacked and slaughtered them. The silence of death would follow.

A Warning of Judgment

> *8:4 Hear this, you that trample on the needy, and bring to ruin the poor of the land,*

The fact that Amos was still speaking God's message to the people meant that God was giving them a further opportunity to repent. He once more addressed his message to rich oppressors, who forced the poor to sell their land at low cost. Many were forced to sell themselves into slavery; others died from want and poverty. In this way they "trampled on the needy".

> *8:5 saying, "When will the new moon be over so that we may sell grain; and the sabbath, so that we may offer wheat for sale? We will make the ephah small and the shekel great, and practice deceit with false balances,*

Although the observance of religious days and festivals continued in the northern kingdom, they were endured with some reluctance. The people's hearts were so far from God that instead of honouring and worshipping Him, and finding joy in His holy days, they were impatient for them to be over. God was getting in the way of what they considered to be more important matters.

Are we in danger of the same thing today? What is our attitude to the worship of God and to the meetings in His house that are meant for Divine service? Is the time we give to the service of the Lord given willingly or grudgingly? Are we impatient to get away from it so that we can spend the day on our own pleasures and interests? How many today would we rather be out shopping than worshipping in the presence of God? Or gossiping rather than serving Christ? Perhaps our modern attitude is not altogether different to that of the people in Amos' time - an attitude of hypocrisy.

They preferred to be out selling their grain at dishonest prices, cheating the customer by giving him less than he ought to receive whilst charging him extra for the privilege of being swindled. These cheats would give you ¾ kilogram and tell you it was a full kilogram, using dishonest weights and weighing scales ("making the ephah small" - an ephah was the unit of measurement then, today we would use the kilogram). The silver coins used for payment were also weighed in these scales, with the weight of one shekel on one side and the coin on the other. By increasing the shekel weight, the already cheated customer was then overcharged - a double fraud!

> 8:6 buying the poor for silver and the needy for a pair of sandals, and selling the sweepings of the wheat."

They were intent on increasing their fortune at the expense of others. Not only did they make slaves of their brother Israelites, but they paid them a very low wage for their services. After they had paid them, they recouped most of their money by selling the workers low quality grain, which was barely fit to eat, at an extortionate price.

> 8:7 The LORD has sworn by the pride of Jacob: Surely I will never forget any of their deeds.

With an oath, God promised never to forget this crime of oppressing the poor, or any of their other evil deeds - an oath taken in His own name, "the pride of Jacob". The NKJV™ has "the excellency of Jacob" or Jacob's king.

> 8:8 Shall not the land tremble on this account, and everyone mourn who lives in it, and all of it rise like the Nile, and be tossed about and sink again, like the Nile of Egypt?

God will send terrible judgment. Using the symbols of earthquake and flood, God shows how the nation will be punished. The River Nile in Egypt would often flood its banks, causing devastation. In a similar way, the invading armies of Assyria would devastate the land and its people, leaving the survivors to mourn bitterly.

> 8:9 On that day, says the Lord GOD, I will make the sun go down at noon, and darken the earth in broad daylight.

It is by no means certain that the prophet literally means that the day of the invasion would coincide with the darkening of the sun (though Beeley points out that a solar eclipse did occur on 15th June 763 BCE, near the time of Amos' ministry). Amos uses this figure to signify the awful grief caused by this disaster.

The words of Amos may, however, be prophetic concerning our Lord Jesus Christ. "On that day" could signify the most important day in history - the day when Christ took away the sin of the world as He hung on the cross. As the Son of God suffered God's wrath and punishment for sin in our place, the whole earth was darkened from midday until 3 p.m. *(Luke 23:44–45)*. This was no solar eclipse, since Passover was always at the time of the full moon. It was a supernatural darkness like that felt in Egypt *(Exodus 10:21–23)*. God saw fit to draw a curtain over His Son's suffering, which was both too sacred and too dreadful for us to look upon.

> 8:10 I will turn your feasts into mourning, and all your songs into lamentation; I will bring sackcloth on all loins, and baldness

> on every head; I will make it like the mourning for an only son, and the end of it like a bitter day.

Since Israel indulged in pagan revelry, God would turn their joy to mourning and their singing into misery. Fine clothes would give place to sackcloth and heads would be shaved - signs of grief and mourning. The bitterness of those days would be like mourning for the death of an only son.

> 8:11 The time is surely coming, says the Lord GOD, when I will send a famine on the land; not a famine of bread, or a thirst for water, but of hearing the words of the LORD.

Since the people had hardened their hearts and refused to listen to God's word, God would prevent them from hearing His voice. He had nothing more to say to them. Since they did not appreciate His word, they would learn its value by the loss of it.

Ray Beeley says, *"This is the most disastrous thing which can befall a nation,"* since, without the word of God, Israel would have, *"No Divine law to regulate its life. No calling to repentance and spiritual and moral purity. No promises to encourage and sustain. Though men do not realise it, this is tragedy indeed, for when the word is withdrawn men both lose hope and cast off restraint."*

Throughout the world today the word of God is being widely ignored - especially by those with power and influence. In Great Britain and throughout Europe laws are being made contrary to the law of God. There are many who suppose that there can be no moral absolutes, and so reject the authority of the Bible as the inspired and infallible word of God, replacing its teachings with their own "morality". Such people go so far as to describe the teachings of the Bible as "immoral". For example, when the Bible warns against sex before marriage, this is supposedly "damaging to the normal sexual health and development of young people". "They must learn how to express their sexuality in a way that feels right to them", they say - and reject the all-wise voice of the One who made man and woman in the beginning. The Bible says *"train up a child in the way he should go"*, but increasingly the moderate and loving corporal punishment of one's own children is being incorrectly labelled as "child abuse".

What will be the result of this rejection of God's word? One day, His pleading voice will fall silent. Men who refuse to hear will one day find that there is no more opportunity to repent *(Proverbs 1:24–30; Isaiah 55:6)*. God's Spirit will not always strive with man. Today He gives us opportunity to repent. We may not have tomorrow. That is why the scripture says *"behold, now is the accepted time; now is the day of salvation." (2 Corinthians 6:2)*.

This does not apply merely to individuals, but to whole nations. God withdraws His blessing and protection from any nation which ignores His word. Perhaps the only reason that Great Britain has not already been overwhelmed with disaster is that there are faithful people among its citizens who do not cease to mourn the ungodliness in our land and appeal in prayer to Almighty God on behalf of it.

As God's people in a wicked and corrupt generation, we must continue to shine as lights in the world and persevere in the all-important work of making the sinner's Saviour known to men, preaching the gospel to every creature. What is needed in our land today is not a change of government but a change of heart, and this can only be achieved as men and women repent, believe the gospel and are born again of God's Holy Spirit.

> 8:12 They shall wander from sea to sea, and from north to east; they shall run to and fro, seeking the word of the LORD, but they shall not find it.

To Israel, Amos says that men will realise too late what they have lost. When they look for God's word they will not find it. All He has left to say is embodied in His judgment. As Beeley says, *"God is sovereign as to when and to whom he offers his word: we cannot afford to neglect it"*.

> 8:13 In that day the beautiful young women and the young men shall faint for thirst.

The beautiful young women and strong young men will faint from thirst. This may well be a literal result of the siege of Samaria.

> 8:14 Those who swear by Ashimah of Samaria, and say, "As your god lives, O Dan," and, "As the way of Beer-sheba lives"-- they shall fall, and never rise again.

The root of all the nation's sin and ungodliness was idolatry. They would fall never to rise since they spurned the living and true God, worshipping instead the golden calves in Dan and Beersheba.

How many men and women today worship other gods without realising it? The existence of a national lottery is just one evidence that the god of gambling and greed is worshipped. The filth and lust, dirty jokes, irreverence and blasphemy toward God that is all over our television screens demonstrates that as a nation we live far from God.

Christians should remember the exhortation of scripture:

"Come out of her, my people, so that you do not take part in her sins, and so that you do not share in her plagues; (Revelation 18:4)

If we become ensnared in the ungodliness around us, we shall be in danger of the judgment of God ourselves and the Bible makes clear what that punishment shall be *(see Revelation 21:8).*

Amos 9:1-15. No Escape—But a Saviour Promised

The Temple at Bethel Destroyed

> 9:1 I saw the LORD standing beside the altar, and he said: Strike the capitals until the thresholds shake, and shatter them on the heads of all the people; and those who are left I will kill with the sword; not one of them shall flee away, not one of them shall escape.

Amos saw the Lord standing near the altar of the temple in Bethel which, though consecrated to the worship of God, had been used as a centre for idolatry.

As the people were gathered to worship their pagan god, the Lord commanded the capitals or lintels holding up the roof be struck and the supporting beams be broken, bringing the whole building crashing down on the worshippers, inflicting death and serious injury - "cutting them in the head".

The vision indicates the destruction of the whole system of idolatrous worship.

God is long-suffering, but when His wrath comes it is both terrible and inescapable. The vision refers not only to those worshippers gathered, but the whole nation whose practice of idolatry had provoked His wrath. The sword of the Assyrian army would be the instrument of Divine punishment against the people. No one would be able to avoid it; attempts of escape would be futile.

No Escape From God's Judgment

> *9:2 Though they dig into Sheol, from there shall my hand take them; though they climb up to heaven, from there I will bring them down.*

When God has determined to judge, there can be no obstacle to His will being done. If men hid themselves in the deepest caves of the earth, God would lay His hands on them. If they climbed the highest mountain and even reached heaven itself, they would be taken and brought down.

> *9:3 Though they hide themselves on the top of Carmel, from there I will search out and take them; and though they hide from my sight at the bottom of the sea, there I will command the sea-serpent, and it shall bite them.*

If they hid among the caves of Mount Carmel, God would search them out that they might face His judgment. The language used is of course poetic and figurative. God has no need to search in order to find anyone for He knows all things. Similarly, no one was able to hide at the bottom of the sea, but if they did, God could easily command a creature of the deep to pursue and destroy them. In other words, there is simply no place to hide from God.

> *9:4 And though they go into captivity in front of their enemies, there I will command the sword, and it shall kill them; and I will fix my eyes on them for harm and not for good.*

Surrendering to their enemies to be taken as captives would not preserve their lives since God had purposed to kill them. The great lesson for today is this, where can any of us hide from the day of judgment? The answer is nowhere. Even death offers no hiding place for impenitent rebels. At the final judgment, death and the grave will give up the dead who are in it and all shall stand, resurrected in their bodies, to be judged by God for the things they had done during their lives *(Revelation 20:11–15).*

God had warned the people to repent for many years through the voice of His prophets, but they had not listened. It is a terrible thing for people to continue to spurn grace until no more grace can be offered.

> *9:5 The Lord, GOD of hosts, he who touches the earth and it melts, and all who live in it mourn, and all of it rises like the Nile, and sinks again, like the Nile of Egypt;*

God's judgment is often associated with His power. He has only to touch the earth and it shakes with a mighty earthquake. Indeed, one day by His word the heaven and earth shall flee away and there will be found no place for them. But that is a future time. In Amos' day, God's punishment of Israel would be as overpowering as the flooding of the mighty river Nile, causing death and mourning, not in isolated towns, but throughout the whole nation.

> *9:6 who builds his upper chambers in the heavens, and founds his vault upon the earth; who calls for the waters of the sea, and pours them out upon the surface of the earth--the LORD is his name.*

In a similar utterance, Isaiah declares *"heaven is my throne and the earth is my footstool" (Isaiah 66:1).*

God's greatness extends throughout the material universe and also far beyond it. Heaven and earth are but the beginnings of His power and are not in themselves able to contain Him.

God has power over nature, as we see in this graphic description of the water cycle. Once, men may have thought that God sent the rain directly from heaven. Scientists later gave a more natural explanation, that through evaporation and condensation there is a continual cycle of rain. But the truth is far more glorious for, as Amos explains, God is the mind and power behind such natural processes and takes as much care over them as if He were watering the earth by hand. All natural processes find their origin in God and continue to be utterly dependent on Him for their continuance. He is Lord with absolute power over all other powers, for whatever other powers exist, they merely derive their power from Him *(1 Timothy 6:15)*.

Misplaced Trust

> 9:7 Are you not like the Ethiopians to me, O people of Israel? says the LORD. Did I not bring Israel up from the land of Egypt, and the Philistines from Caphtor and the Arameans from Kir?

Despite continued warnings because of their sin, Israel trusted in the fact that they were the covenant people of God. They considered themselves better and superior to other nations because of their unique relationship with the Lord. Yet this covenant relationship did not come about because of Israel's righteousness or superiority. God did not choose them because they were better than others, but because of His own purpose and grace, that they might keep His laws. Since they had not kept His laws, how were they better than any other nation?

God had been involved in the affairs of all nations, not just Israel. The Syrians and Philistines had attracted just as much concern from God although they had not been privileged to receive the revelation which was entrusted to Israel.

God had to teach His people that their privileged relationship would not lead Him to show favouritism, especially when the relationship had already broken down.

Scattering and Sifting

> *9:8 The eyes of the Lord GOD are upon the sinful kingdom, and I will destroy it from the face of the earth--except that I will not utterly destroy the house of Jacob, says the LORD.*

God's penetrating gaze was fixed on the sinful kingdom to remove it from being a nation. The cessation of the nation of Israel should be viewed in the context of its existing separately from Judah. It would never again have another king, for as we see later in this chapter, there would be no king until the "the descendant of David" reigns over all twelve tribes and the whole earth. In destroying the nation, God would not destroy all the people, for He would keep His promise to Abraham, Isaac and Jacob. So a remnant would remain, that God might fulfil His promise to give a Saviour for the world through the Hebrew nation.

> *9:9 For lo, I will command, and shake the house of Israel among all the nations as one shakes with a sieve, but no pebble shall fall to the ground.*

The nation would be sifted like corn by many troubles, scattered throughout many foreign countries. The purpose of sifting is to remove the worthless chaff and to safely collect and store the grain. So, the grain, that is the godly, will by no means be lost. As Beeley says, *"Though judgment is universal in its outreach it is individual in its discernment".*

Jesus assures us of the security of the godly when He says that in spite of trouble or death *"not a hair of your head shall perish"* (Luke 21:18) and we will never be lost for *"no man can pluck them out of my hand"* (John 10:28).

> *9:10 All the sinners of my people shall die by the sword, who say, "Evil shall not overtake or meet us."*

Sinners, rebels who refuse to repent, think that no harm will come to them because of their sin. They like to think that they are immune to punishment and in this self-deception they continue in sin. But they will be destroyed.

The Restoration of the Davidic Kingship

> *9:11 On that day I will raise up the booth of David that is fallen, and repair its breaches, and raise up its ruins, and rebuild it as in the days of old;*

Here is one of the great Messianic prophecies in the Old Testament. God is speaking of a day when the kingdom would be restored to the house of David. Remember that Israel was split into two parts at this time, Israel and Judah, and David's descendants ruled only Judah. Later still, Judah would be captured and the kingly line lose all its power and influence. In this prophecy God refers to a day when the whole kingdom of Israel and Judah would be reunited under the leadership of a new king, whose kingdom would be exalted and blessed, just as David's had been, so that all the people would rally to him.

> *9:12 in order that they may possess the remnant of Edom and all the nations who are called by my name, says the LORD who does this.*

Not only the Jewish nation, but people from all other nations (rather than "the remnant of Edom", it should read "the rest of mankind") would gather to this exalted king and own Him as their own Lord and Master, so that both Jew and Gentile, by accepting the Lordship of that king would become God's own people. This king of course is none other than the Lord Jesus Christ. The fact of His eternal kingship was announced by the angel before his birth *(Luke 1:32–33)*. It was accepted by the Wise Men *(Matthew 2:2)* and confirmed by other scriptures *(e.g. Matthew 21:5)*.

About the matter of Christ becoming king over a "greater nation" made up of both Jews and Gentiles who believe in him, Jesus said much *(e.g. John 10:16)*. Although it took time to sink in, James had an understanding of this prophecy in *(Acts 15:14–17)*. It is explained briefly by Paul in Ephesians *(e.g. Ephesians 3:6)*. Christ will one day be king over all the earth for He is King of Kings and Lord of Lords *(Psalm 2:8; Revelation 12:5)*.

> 9:13 The time is surely coming, says the LORD, when the one who plows shall overtake the one who reaps, and the treader of grapes the one who sows the seed; the mountains shall drip sweet wine, and all the hills shall flow with it.

This day of restoration would be accompanied by such blessings as are here figuratively described. Imagine the scene painted by Amos: a harvest so abundant that before it is gathered in, autumn arrives and new seed must be planted. Last year's grapes are still being pressed when the new crop is sown and the mountains run with rivers of wine. Such is the abundant blessing which God has outpoured on His people through Christ *(Ephesians 1:3)*.

9:14–15 I will restore the fortunes of my people Israel, and they shall rebuild the ruined cities and inhabit them; they shall plant vineyards and drink their wine, and they shall make gardens and eat their fruit. I will plant them upon their land, and they shall never again be plucked up out of the land that I have given them, says the LORD your God.

Yet a day of material blessing and restoration is also promised for the nation of Israel, under their new king. He promises to bring them back from captivity and to settle them again in their land, where they will rebuild the waste cities and live in them, enjoying the produce of the land.

Since God himself would give them back the land, no one could ever remove them from it, for his purpose is immutable. What a great comfort this gives to us who are saved by His grace! If God has once brought us into His loving favour, no one can ever remove us from it. *"If God be for us, who can be against us?" (Romans 8:31).*

God's promise embraces a series of events. Some Israelites may have returned to the land at various times after the Assyrian war, and a greater number during the reign of Cyrus. But the nation was to be scattered once again by the Romans so that for nearly 2000 years there was no such nation as Israel. Today, God has given them their own land and Israel is a nation again. Are they living in abundant blessing? No, their return to the land is only a beginning of the fulfilment of this promise. When Jesus Christ comes again and is welcomed by Israel, "a nation will be born in a day". Then the fullness of the promised Messianic blessing will be ushered in and Christ will reign on earth for a thousand years, a time of unimaginable blessing.

Bibliography

1. Tatford, Frederick A. 1974. *Prophet of Social Injustice - An Exposition of Amos.* Eastbourne: Prophetic Witness Publishing House

2. Beeley, Ray. 1970. *Amos.* London: The Banner of Truth Trust.

3. *The Living Bible.* 1974. Tyndale.

4. Thiele, *Edwin. 1951. The Mysterious Numbers of the Hebrew Kings.* New York: Macmillan.

BV - #0028 - 240326 - C0 - 216/138/5 - PB - 9781910942192 - Gloss Lamination